The Usborne

Big Book of Trucks

Written by Megan Cullis

Illustrated by Mike Byrne

Designed by Stephen Wright

Truck expert: Steve Williams

Recovery trucks

These trucks tow broken-down vehicles to garages or mechanics where they can be fixed.

This **recovery truck** is lifting up a broken-down **dropside truck**.

Cable

This sling supports the truck.

This metal arm is called a **boom**. It's so strong it can lift two trucks the size of this one.

Metal legs called **outriggers** are lowered to steady the truck.

This **winch** winds the cable to lift and lower the boom.

Cab, where the driver sits

Each car is strapped to the deck to stop it from slipping.

Tank

Bed

Pick-up trucks, like this one, are often used to carry building materials.

This **car transporter** is carrying 10 cars on different levels.

The decks can move up and down so the cars can be driven on and off.

Chain hand rails

Road trucks

Bed

A **flatbed truck**
has no sides or roof, so it
can carry very large items
such as mobile homes.

A **pick-up truck**
has an uncovered part
at the back, called a bed,
where the load is kept.

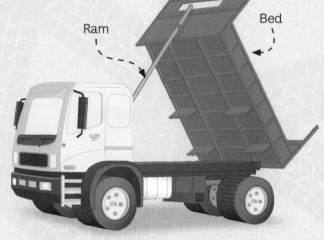

Ram

Bed

A **tipper truck** delivers sand and
gravel. An arm called a ram lifts
up the bed at the back of the
truck to pour out the load.

Tankers, like this one,
carry liquids, powders
and gases.

Container

Pipe

A **container truck**
transports huge metal
boxes, called containers, to
and from docks or ports.

A **gully emptier**
uses a long pipe to suck
waste water out of drains
and up into its tank.

A **car transporter** delivers
lots of cars to garages and
showrooms. Some can carry
as many as 12 large cars.

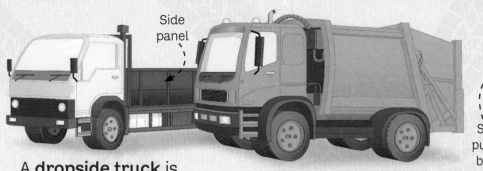

Side panel

A **dropside truck** is loaded by unbolting and lowering each side panel.

A **refuse truck** collects waste and takes it to a landfill site.

Side pulled back

A **curtainsider** has sides made of soft waterproof material, which slide open.

Decks

A **livestock truck** transports farm animals on different levels, called decks.

Flashing sign

A **highway maintenance truck** carries workers and supplies to mend roads.

A **dry bulk tanker** transports dry loads such as flour, grain or fertilizer.

The tractor unit holds the engine.

Semi-trailers

This truck is so long it's called a **road train**. It's used for long-distance journeys.

This **road train** is made up of three separate compartments called semi-trailers. Each one is as long as a bus.

The truck's engine has to be very powerful to pull this much weight.

Tankers are difficult to drive because the load inside can slosh around.

This loaded tanker is as heavy as 13 pick-up trucks.

Most road trains are so huge they can't drive through towns and cities. They can't turn corners easily and would block the roads.

LONG LOAD

This **tanker** carries fuel. But others transport food, such as milk or flour.

Inside the tanker there are separate compartments, so it can carry different loads.

This tanker carries enough fuel in its tank to fill over 500 cars.

Higher and higher

These trucks lift loads up high using long metal arms, called booms.

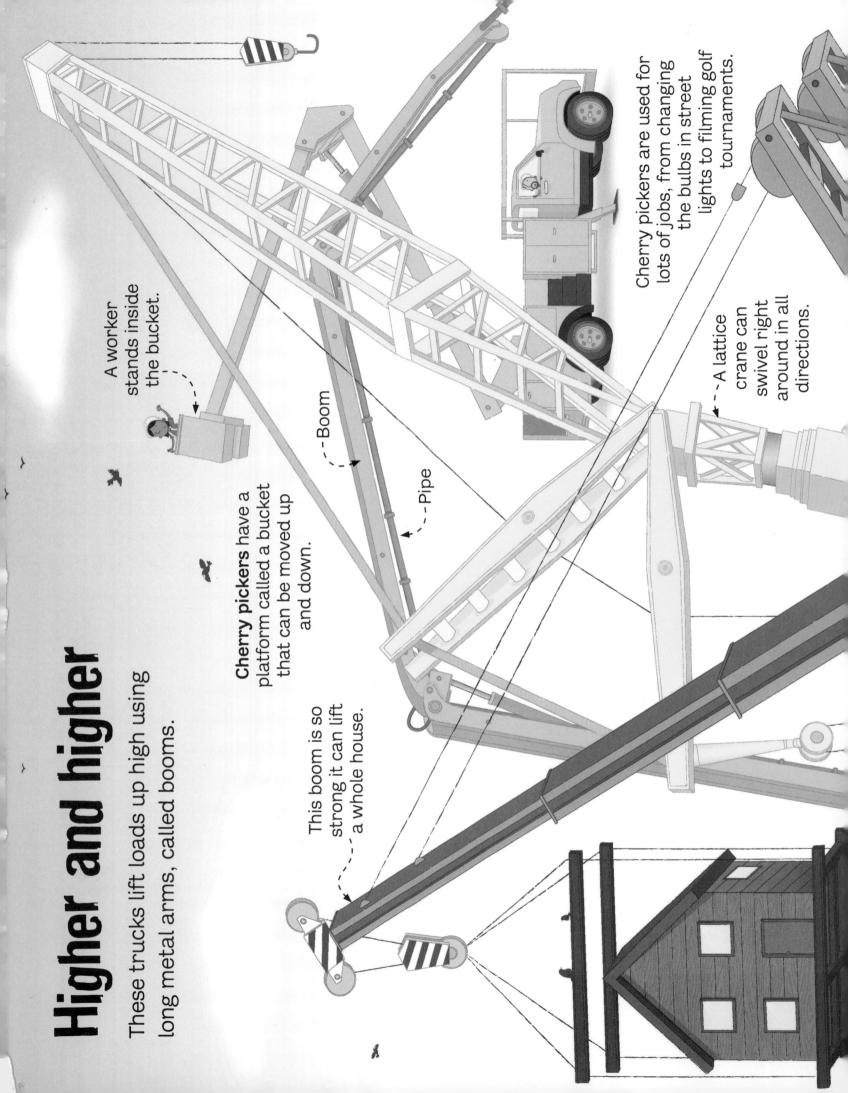

A worker stands inside the bucket.

Cherry pickers have a platform called a bucket that can be moved up and down.

Boom

Pipe

This boom is so strong it can lift a whole house.

Cherry pickers are used for lots of jobs, from changing the bulbs in street lights to filming golf tournaments.

A lattice crane can swivel right around in all directions.

Heavy weights keep the truck balanced as it lifts a load.

Outriggers steady the truck.

This boom can reach as high as an 11 storey building.

A **concrete pump truck** pumps out concrete into tall buildings, through a long pipe attached to its boom.

This **lattice boom crane truck** is used to lift very heavy things, often made of steel or concrete.

A **mobile telescopic boom truck** has a very tall boom made up of several sliding parts.

Mining trucks

Giant mining trucks are used to transport loads from mines and quarries. They are often so huge they have to be carried in pieces and put together at the mine.

This **heavy hauler dump truck** is a Liebherr T 282B. It moves massive loads of rocks from the mine to a storage area.

Cab

The truck is so big it's about the size of a small house.

Metal grills protect the driver from falling rocks.

Long stairway to reach the cab

Bucket

This **skid steer loader** scoots between big mining machines. It has a small bucket to lift light loads.

This bucket is so big and strong it could lift 13 elephants.

A **mining scraper** scrapes earth from the ground and loads it into a bowl.

This **rubber-tyred wheel loader** is a LeTourneau L-2350. It uses a huge bucket to load piles of rocks into the heavy hauler dump truck.

Each wheel is nearly 4m (13ft) tall – and as heavy as three cars.

Cab

The transporter bed can be moved up and down to make it easier to load and unload.

This **ALMA antenna transporter** transports massive radio antennas.

It has 28 wheels to help it move into awkward positions.

The driver controls the transporter from inside this cab.

This dump box holds
enough rocks to build
a small house.

Heavy loads

Heavy duty transporter trucks have powerful engines and lots of wheels, but they're so heavy they can only move very slowly.

A **rail transporter** carries train carriages that aren't in use.

It travels at 6km (4 miles) per hour. That's no faster than a person jogging.

This **rocket transporter** is used to haul space rocket engines to the rocket launch pad.

This rocket engine is heavier than an entire jumbo jet.

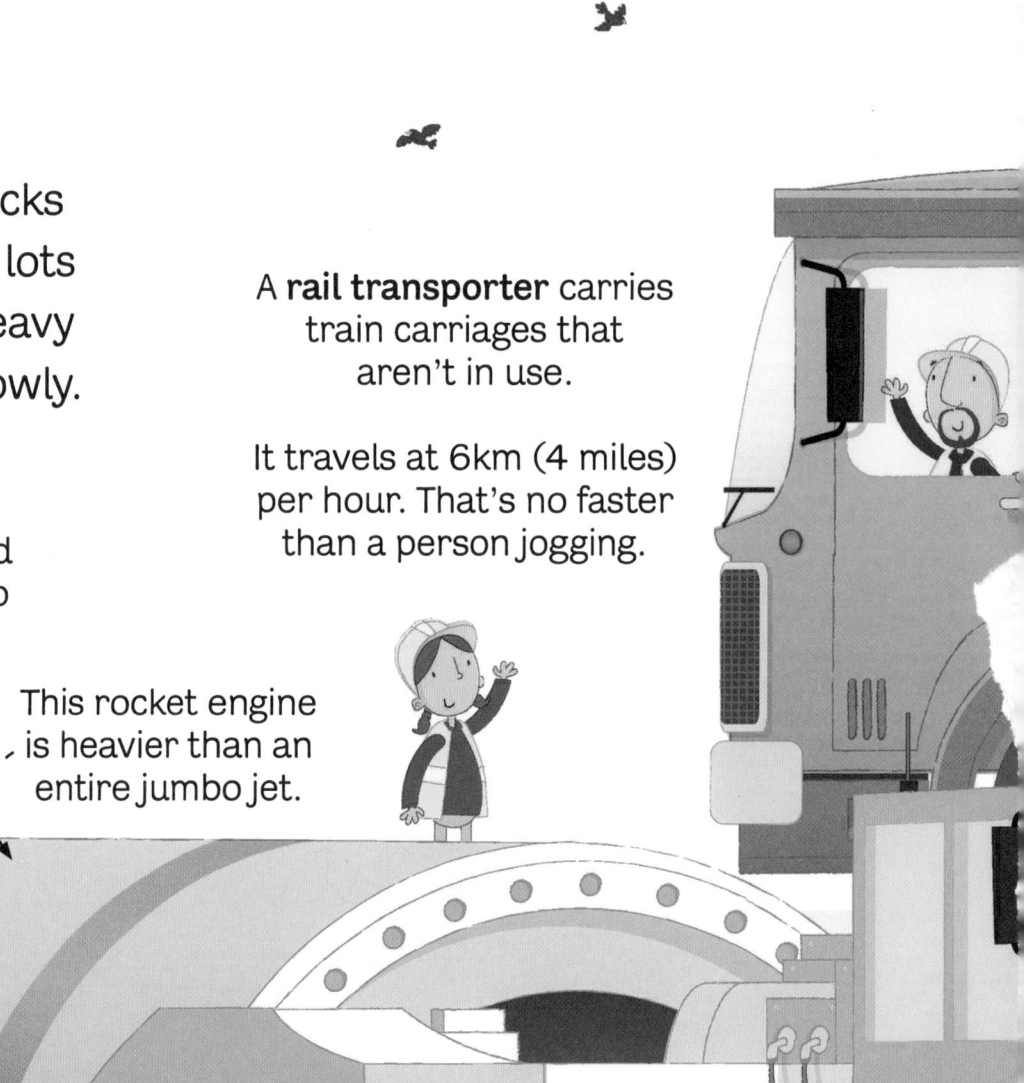

This deck supports the weight of the engine.

The driver uses controls to lower the bowl and scrape up the earth.

This radio antenna is used by scientists to look at things in space.

The weight of the train is spread out over 40 wheels.

This vast yellow truck is one of only two ALMA transporters in the world. It climbs up mountains in South America.

It travels at 12km (7 miles) per hour – about as fast as a trotting horse.

A built-in crane can pick up overturned tanks.

Extendable boom

These wheels are over 2m (6ft) tall – that's taller than most men.

Logging trucks, like this one, have tall metal prongs on each side to keep the logs secure.

This **army recovery truck** can rescue tanks trapped in heavy snow or mud.

This **log stacker** loads logs onto a logging truck.

This **utility terrain vehicle** is so tough it can drive through mud, snow and flooded ground.

Extreme trucks

Trucks like these work in tricky conditions – such as snow and ice, mud or sand, and uneven steep slopes.

A **utility terrain vehicle** is handy for climbing up steep slopes.

An **army truck** carries soldiers and supplies across battlefields.

Canvas roof

Snow chute

Spinning drum

This **snow blower** has a spinning drum which clears heavy snow.

An **off-road pick-up truck** drives on bumpy roads and rocky tracks without any trouble.

A **log stacker** picks up logs in muddy forests using a strong metal grab.

Metal grab

Big, wide wheels help to grip bumpy ground.

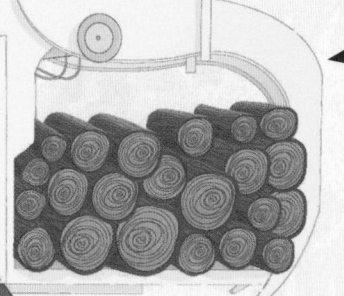

An **army recovery truck** tows broken-down army tanks out of danger.

Roof rack

A **mountain rescue truck** carries a rescue team to emergencies on the top of mountains. It can tow other vehicles to safety.

This ladder stretches up to 10m (32ft) long.

An **all-terrain fire truck** transports fire fighters, a water tank and pump to put out fires in forests and rough country.

Blade

A **snow plough** scrapes snow off roads using a big tilted blade.

A **logging truck** transports heavy piles of logs from forests high up in the mountains.

This giant **snow blower** is pumping snow 60m (200ft) into the air – that's higher than a 16 storey building.

It clears snow off airport runways, to allow planes to take off and land.

A powerful spinning blade inside this drum churns up the snow.

Metal prongs

The grab opens up like a claw. This one's wide enough to pick up a bus.

Truck sports

Some trucks are built especially to take part in sports events and competitions.

Monster trucks can perform amazing stunts, such as crushing cars with their vast wheels.

This monster truck is called BIGFOOT® #5. It's almost 5m (16ft) tall – that's about as tall as four cars on top of one another.

These engines were taken from fighter planes.

This **pro-jet truck** is powered by three jet engines. It races overhead planes at speeds of 320km (198 miles) per hour.

Metal springs stop the truck from being damaged as it bounces over mounds.

Deep grooves help the wheels grip the ground.

This massive wheel is heavier than 50 car wheels.

This **off-road racing truck** races on rough and bumpy tracks and up steep hills.

The truck goes so fast it uses parachutes to help it slow down at the end of a race.

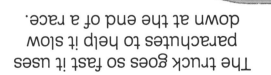

Biggest, tallest, fastest...

The world's HEAVIEST monster truck is **BIGFOOT®#5**. It weighs 14 tons – the same as 10 cars.

The BIGGEST kind of truck is a heavy hauler dump truck, like this **Liebherr T 282B**. It's as big as a house.

The wheels are so heavy, it takes three hours to change each one.

The TALLEST trucks are telescopic crane trucks like this **Liebherr LTM 11200-9.1**. It can be used to build television masts.

The LONGEST ever **road train** was put together just to beat a world record. It had 112 semi-trailers, and drove only 100m (328ft).

The road train was over 1km (nearly a mile) long – seven times longer than most passenger trains.

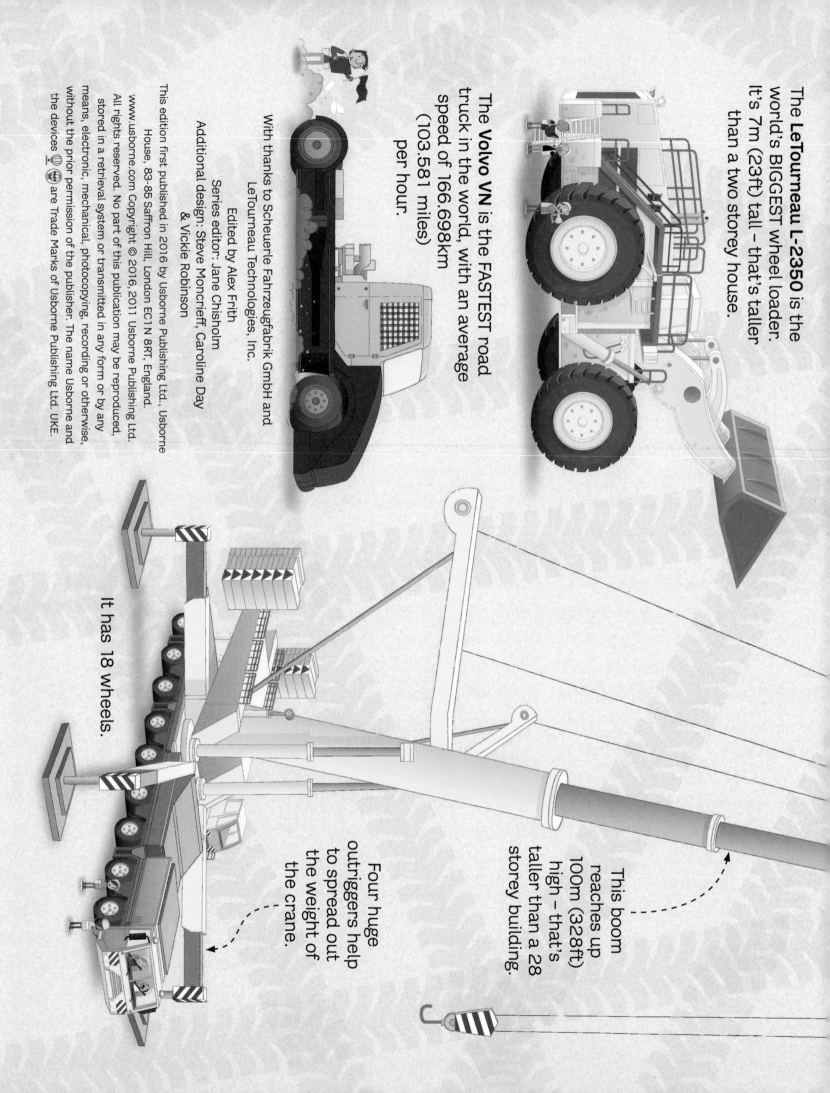

The **LeTourneau L-2350** is the world's BIGGEST wheel loader. It's 7m (23ft) tall – that's taller than a two storey house.

The **Volvo VN** is the FASTEST road truck in the world, with an average speed of 166.698km (103.581 miles) per hour.

This boom reaches up 100m (328ft) high – that's taller than a 28 storey building.

Four huge outriggers help to spread out the weight of the crane.

It has 18 wheels.

With thanks to Scheuerle Fahrzeugfabrik GmbH and LeTourneau Technologies, Inc.

Edited by Alex Frith

Series editor: Jane Chisholm

Additional design: Steve Moncrieff, Caroline Day & Vickie Robinson